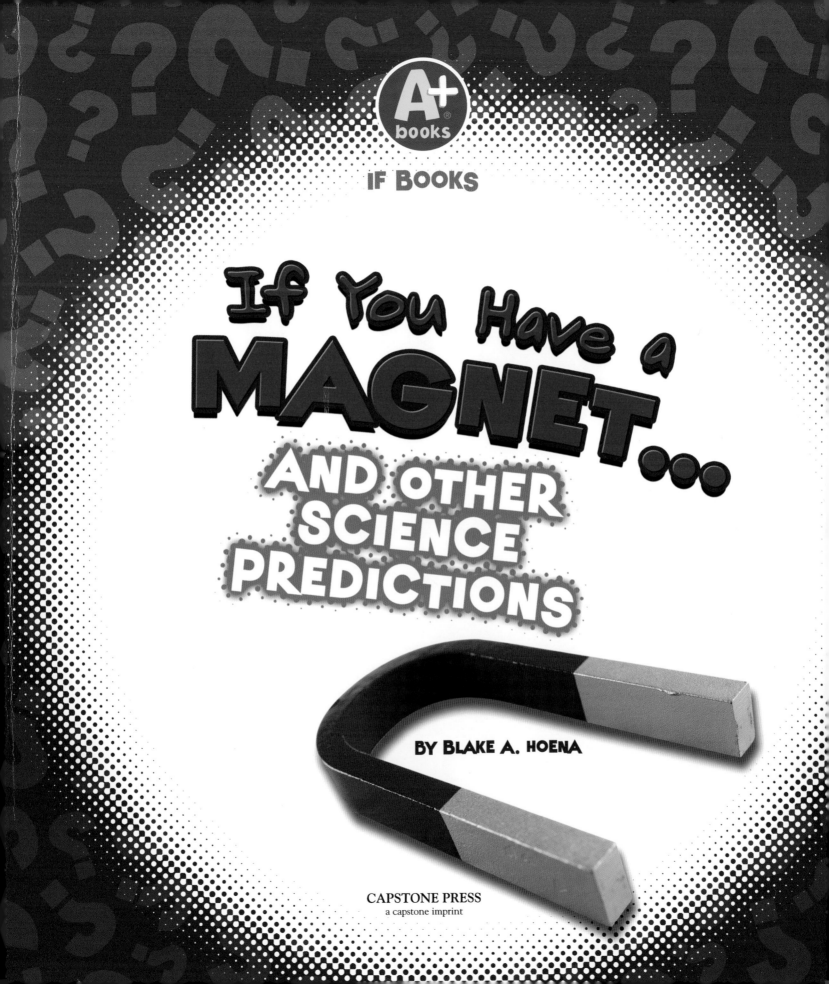

A+ books

IF BOOKS

# If You Have a MAGNET...
## AND OTHER SCIENCE PREDICTIONS

BY BLAKE A. HOENA

CAPSTONE PRESS
a capstone imprint

The world is full of wonders—the sounds we hear and the sights we see. But if you watch closely, you can use science to predict what will happen. Want to give it a try?

Magnets aren't magic, even
though they perform a neat trick.
They pick up metal objects like
cars and paperclips.
Now what would happen if you
hold a magnet over an apple?

ANSWER

Nothing—apples aren't made of metal. Magnets cannot pick up living objects like you or a cat or an apple. But they can pick up certain metal objects like nails and pins.

Ice is made of water, and so is fog. You can't poke your finger through ice because it's a solid. But you can walk right through fog. What would happen if you stuck your hand into water?

ANSWER

Water is a liquid, so you can move your hand through it. It's pretty easy to walk through fog, a gas form of water. But it's more difficult to walk through water.

Did you know that light travels in a straight line? **ZIP!!!** Faster than you or even me. Light moves quickly, but it cannot pass through solid objects, like a door or a brick.

So what happens when you put your hand in front of a light?

ANSWER

You create a shadow. Shadows are created when objects block the path of light.

You can't move without energy, and your body gets its energy from food. Food fuels your muscles, so you have the energy to run and jump, swing and skip. But what would happen if you missed breakfast?

ANSWER

Your body would have less energy and you'd feel tired. A healthy snack during the day is a great way to keep up your energy levels.

Kayakers use paddles to push through the water. A motorboat's motor propels a speedboat through the waves. What would happen if a gust of wind filled a sailboat's sails?

ANSWER

The sailboat would move forward. The force of the wind blowing against a sailboat's sails is how it moves through the water.

When the sun beats down on lakes and ponds, they begin to empty. The water evaporates and rises to form clouds. When those clouds loom dark and stormy overhead, what happens next?

ANSWER

Rain falls to fill up the lakes and ponds again. Water evaporates to form clouds and then falls back to the Earth as rain. This is called the water cycle.

Objects have three states: solid, liquid, or gas. Water is liquid. During the cold of winter, rain puddles freeze into ice, a solid.

But during the heat of summer, what happens to the puddle?

ANSWER

It will disappear. The water evaporates and turns into water vapor, a gas.

What goes up must come down. That's the law of gravity. If you tossed up a rock, it will eventually land on the ground. If you kicked a ball, it too will come right back down. But what if there was no gravity, and you leaped into the air?

You'd float, like an astronaut in space. Gravity is what keeps people (and everything else!) on the ground.

See the moon in the night sky? Sometimes the moon seems to shrink. Tonight, the moon looks like a tiny silver sliver of itself. Will the moon simply disappear forever? What will happen next?

The moon doesn't really disappear or get smaller. As the moon circles Earth, we can only see the part that is lit by the sun. These are the moon phases.

The stars are pinpricks of twinkling light in the night sky. They seem small because they are so very far away.

What if one of those stars moved into our solar system?

ANSWER

We'd have two suns.
Our sun is a star, just
like the others in the
night sky.

Heat is a type of energy, and everything reacts differently to heat. If you put water in the hot sun, it will evaporate. Really hot sun will melt a plastic toy. If it's that hot, what would happen to a hot dog?

ANSWER

It would cook. We use heat to cook food. In fact, people actually make "solar ovens" that use the sun to cook hot dogs and other food.

Sound is caused by tiny vibrations traveling to your ear. If you tap on a desk, it vibrates and you hear a sound. If you tap on a drum, you also hear a sound. What happens if you **BANG** on the drum?

ANSWER

You hear a loud sound. Tapping on a drum causes small vibrations, so you hear a quiet sound. Banging on it creates large vibrations, so the sound is louder.

Plop! If you toss a coin in a swimming pool, it sinks to the bottom. Throw a sock in, and it floats for a bit, then sinks. If you drop an oak leaf in the pool, it floats on the water's surface.

If a 70,000-ton (63,500 metric-ton) piece of metal slides into the ocean, what do you think will happen?

ANSWER

It depends on the shape of the metal! If it is a cruise ship, it will float. Cruise ships can be as long as three football fields and taller than the Statue of Liberty, but their special shape allows them to float.

How many of your predictions were correct? Did you know a lot about science or learn something new? Studying science helps you better understand the world around you. Try making your own science predictions and see if they come true!

# GLOSSARY

**energy**—the power to do things

**evaporate**—to change from a liquid to a gas

**force**—movement or strength that changes the movement of an object

**gas**—something that is not solid or liquid and does not have a definite shape

**gravity**—a force that pulls objects together

**liquid**—something that is wet and can be poured, such as water

**magnet**—a piece of metal that attracts iron or steel

**shadow**—the dark shape made when something blocks light

**solid**—something that holds its shape

**vibration**—a fast movement back and forth

**water vapor**—water in gas form; water vapor is one of many invisible gases in air

# READ MORE

**Burns, Loree Griffin.** *Citizen Scientists: Be a Part of Scientific Discovery from Your Own Backyard.* New York: H. Holt, 2012.

**Vogel, Julia.** *Push and Pull! Learn about Magnets.* Mankato, Minn.: Child's World, 2011.

**Wells, Robert E.** *Why Do Elephants Need the Sun?* Chicago: Albert Whitman & Co., 2012.

# INTERNET SITES

FactHound offers a safe, fun way to find Internet sites related to this book. All of the sites on FactHound have been researched by our staff.

Here's all you do:

Visit *www.facthound.com*

Type in this code: 9781429687201

**Super-cool stuff!** Check out projects, games and lots more at **www.capstonekids.com**

A+ books are published by Capstone Publishers,
1710 Roe Crest Drive, North Mankato, MN 56003
www.capstonepub.com

*Library of Congress Cataloging-in-Publication Data*
Hoena, B. A.
  If you have a magnet ... and other science predictions / by Blake A. Hoena.
    p. cm.—(A+ books. If books)
  Audience: 5-8
  Audience: K to Grade 3
  Summary: "Simple text and full-color photos invite readers to make fun predictions about science"—Provided by publisher.
  Includes bibliographical references.
  ISBN 978-1-4296-8720-1 (library binding)
  ISBN 978-1-4296-9249-6 (paperback)
  ISBN 978-1-62065-193-3 (eBook PDF)
  1. Science—Methodology—Juvenile literature. I. Title.
  Q175.2.H64 2013
  507.2'1—dc23                                    2012008913

**Credits**

Jeni Wittrock, editor; Ted Williams, designer; Svetlana Zhurkin, media researcher; Laura Manthe,
    production specialist

**Photo Credits**

Alamy: Photononstop, 29; Capstone Studio: Karon Dubke, cover, 1, 2, 3 (all), 4, 5, 7, 8, 10, 13, 16, 17, 25, 26; Dreamstime:
Aiyoshi, 20, An Van De Wal, 12, Limeyrunner, 27, Monkey Business Images, 9, Speedo101, 19; NASA, 18, Solar Dynamics
Observatory, 22; Shutterstock: dpaint, 14, Login (question background), throughout, M. Cornelius, 24, Noel Powell, 21, Olga
Lyubkina, 11, Picsfive, 23, Sergey Panychev, 15, ying, 6, Yuriy Chertok, 28

**Note to Parents, Teachers, and Librarians**

This If Book uses full color photographs and fun text to introduce K-2 science concepts in an interactive, predictive format. *If You Have a Magnet . . . And Other Science Predictions* is designed to be read aloud to a pre-reader or to be read independently by an early reader. Photographs help listeners and early readers understand the text and concepts discussed. The book encourages further learning by including the following sections: Glossary, Read More, and Internet Sites. Early readers may need assistance using these features.

Printed in the United States of America in North Mankato, Minnesota.
042012      006682CGF12